CONT

G000295908

See it

Slap bang in the middle of England, Oxford is a city of enviable fortune: stunning architecture, abundant gardens and riverways, academic excellence and cultural richness. A far cry from the oxen grazing ground after which it was named, 'Oxen-ford' today boasts 38 prestigious colleges; a University church and a city cathedral; the ancient Bodleian library; Wren's Sheldonian theatre; and the iconic Radcliffe Camera. Add to this a bevy of prominent museums from the age-old Ashmolean to the oddities of Pitt Rivers and you may find your itinerary a little overwhelming. If you are pushed for time make a beeline for St Mary's churchtower to experience the characteristic splendour of Oxford that the gargoyles gorge themselves on daily.

The formidable Bodleian Library

Ashmolean Museum 3C

Laying claim as Britain's 'oldest public museum' following its opening in 1683, the Ashmolean houses an impressive bounty of art and antiquities collected over time and place. The interlinking theme of 'Crossing Cultures, Crossing Time' pulls together the varied collections including the 39 new galleries created from Rick Mather's new wing in 2009. Highlights include King Alfred's jewel, a Samurai Suit of Armour, Cromwell's death mask, and a deerskin mantle belonging to Pocahontas' father. It also boasts Oxford's first rooftop restaurant (see p.26) which is perfect for a reflective pit stop between exhibit browsing. Adm free. Open 10am-5pm Tue-Sun. Beaumont St, T: 01865 278000, www.ashmolean.org

Bodleian Library 4E

The grand frontage of the Bodleian does little to disclose the immense rabbit warren of tunnels concealed beneath ground containing more than 11 million printed materials on 117 miles of shelving plus a host of other formats. See how the experts cope with this storage nightmare on a variety of guided tours that include the underground tunnels (extended tour only), Convocation House, the magnificent vaulted ceiling of the Divinity School and Duke Humphrey's library. The latter, which doubled as the Hogwart's Library (*see box p.4*), was built in 1444 to originally house the Duke's manuscript collection. Luckily the building and its books have stood up well against the tests of time and appear all but unchanged. In 2015 **Weston Library** on Broad Street (4E) completed its three year refurbishment and now houses the Bodleian's special collections. Its exhibition galleries, shop and café are open to the public. *Adm. Open 9am-5pm Mon-Fri, 9am-4.30pm Sat, 11am-5pm Sun. Check website for* up-to-date guided tour times. Audio tours available in English, French & German. Broad St, T: 01865 287400, www.bodley.ox.ac.uk*

Carfax Tower 4D

Probably the best place to meet in Oxford, the 23-metre-high tower is the last remains of St Martin's church and pretty hard to miss. It is thought that the name Carfax derives from the Saxon's poor pronunciation of the French word *carrefour* meaning crossroads. Look up on the east face and you'll see two quarter boys below the clock-face who hammer the bells every 15 minutes. Inside, climb the 99 steps for reasonable views over the city but pick your time wisely as it can get quite congested on the narrow stairs. *Adm. Open daily 10am-5.30pm (4.30pm in Oct). St Aldate's/Cornmarket St and High St/ Queen St, T: 01865 790522, www.citysightseeingoxford.co.uk*

Modern Art Oxford 5D

Housed in an old brewery warehouse, the MAO has oodles of

Randolph Sculpture Gallery, Ashmolean Museum

Potty for Potter?

For all those die-hard Harry Potter fans out there, what better way to indulge your interests than with a guided tour which visits the key film locations around the city:

Christ Church College's Great Hall (**5E**) = Hogwart's Hall;
Duke Humphrey's Library (**4E**) = Hogwart's Library;
The Divinity School in the Bodleian (**4E**) = Hogwart's Infirmary
Tours depart from the TIC but pre-booking is essential (*see p.28*): *T: 01865 686441, www.visitoxfordandoxfordshire.com*

space in which to cater exhibitions from a host of leading artists including the likes of Tracey Emin and the Chapman brothers, Jake & Dinos. The MAO has a regular programme of events, workshops, contemporary music and film nights. It also boasts a great shop and basement café bolthole, allowing you time-out to fully digest the sights and sounds of the artwork over an existential café latte and slice of carrot cake.

Adm free. Open 11am-6pm Tues-Sat, 12noon-5pm Sun.
30 Pembroke St, T: 01865 722733, www.modernartoxford.org.uk

Oxford Castle Unlocked 5C

After nearly 1000 turbulent years of history the castle has opened its doors to the public allowing you to explore every nook and cranny. Tramp the 101 winding steps up St George's tower to enjoy 360-degree views over the city and if you have children in tow there's also a chance to spot a ghost or two along the way before heading down into the depths of the 900-year-old underground crypt. Final stop is Prisoner D-wing where you can do some time *in the ginger* with the help of truly interactive audiovisual guides that steer you through the changing history of the prison and the lives of its inmates. Get your mugshot taken and if

Oxford Castle behind bars

4

you're feeling particularly sinful you can do some hard labour on the capstan wheel before you go. *Adm. Open daily 10am-5.30pm. 44-46 Oxford Castle, T: 01865 260666, www.oxfordcastleunlocked.co.uk*

Oxford University Museum of Natural History 2E

Follow the tracks of giant *Megalosaurus* and *Cetiosaurus* footprints that stampede their way across the museum's elegant front lawn to reach this 'cathedral to science'. The looming skeleton

Gargoyle or Grotesque?

Spot the difference: gargoyles are on hand to channel or 'gargle' rainwater off the roof through their mouths whereas grotesques are just there to look plain ugly.

cast of *Iguanodon* is on hand to greet you along with a multitude of animal, mineral and insect specimens including crabs collected by Charles Darwin on *The Beagle* and the mummified dodo head that was immortalised in *Alice's*

Bishop keeping watch over Magdalen Bridge

Adventures in Wonderland (see p.14). A free EXPLORE app is also available for download from their website on iOS and Android which gives further detail on all of the four Oxford University Museums. *Adm free. Open daily 10am-5pm. Parks Rd, T: 01865 272950, www.oum.ox.ac.uk*

Pitt Rivers Museum 2E

Here you'll find a museum crammed with a plethora of anthropological

Butterflies at the Oxford University Museum of Natural History

St Mary's Church in springtime

and ethnographic oddities. Display cabinets literally bursting with artefacts — boats hanging from the ceiling and totem poles reaching up to the roof — provide a feast for the eyes and an arrangement little changed since its compilation in 1884. Recent development however, has seen an improved upper gallery housing an impressive weapons display, and there are future plans to upgrade the display case lighting

following an improvement fund award. If the sheer number of artefacts proves daunting then you can pick up a family trail from the information point to help navigate your way through the eclectic mix of shrunken heads and a witch held captive in a glass bottle. *Adm free. Open 10am-4.30pm Tue-Sun & 12noon-4.30pm Mon. Entrance via the Museum of Natural History, South Parks Rd, T: 01865 270927, www.prm.ox.ac.uk*

Radcliffe Camera 4E

Probably the most photographed building in Oxford, the domed Radcliffe Camera or 'Rad Cam' was designed by James Gibb and built in 1737-1749 to house the Radcliffe Science library. It is now part of the Bodleian complex (*see p.3*) although public access is through guided tours only. If you find yourself here around *Encaenia* time (*see p.16*) in June you can observe the gowned honorary

Radcliffe Camera

Blooms on show at the Botanic Garden

degree recipients as they pose for their graduation photos in the square. T: 01865 277224, www.bodley.ox.ac.uk

St Mary the Virgin Church 4E

Adopted as a University church in the 13th-century, St Mary's remains at the hub of University life. If you relish a little drama then enter from the High Street to appreciate the substantial barley sugar columns and decorative carvings that are framed beautifully by almond tree blossom in springtime. Once inside, the real 'must-see' lies 127 steps up the twisting staircase of the tower. If you can tackle this rather steep climb in places, you will be rewarded with *the* best panoramic views over Oxford. *Adm for the tower only. Open daily 9am-5pm (9am-6pm Jul-Aug). Access to tower on Sundays is from 11.30am. High St, T: 01865 279111, www.universitychurch.ox.ac.uk*

The Story Museum 5D

Oxford has always had a strong affinity with story-telling thanks to its famous resident writers like J.R.R. Tolkien, C.S. Lewis *(see p.27)* and Philip Pullman. Now the city has a museum in which to celebrate them. Kids can try their hand at story illustration or dress up and indulge in plenty of story-telling over two floors of changing exhibitions. Further renovation is also ongoing to improve facilities by 2018. *Adm. Open 10am-5pm Tues-Sat, 11am-4pm Sun. 42 Pembroke St, T: 01865 790050, www.storymuseum.org.uk*

University Botanic Garden 5G

These are the 'oldest' botanic gardens in Britain established in

Town vs. Gown

The original odd couple, 'town and gown' share a bloody history that has set the tone for their mutual loathing ever since. It all kicked off on February 10th 1355 after two students complained about some sour wine they were served at the appropriately named Swindlestock Tavern. Instead of taking their complaint to their local ombudsman they took it out on the landlord, throwing a quart pot at his head and beating him to a pulp. Thereafter followed two days of bloody riots, leaving around 63 scholars and 30 locals dead. The King stepped in to quell the fighting but, favouring the scholars, he ordered the Mayor to make 63 townspeople attend an annual mass to pray for the dead scholars' souls and, worse still, pay a penny each for the privilege.

Christ Church College's Tom Tower

1621 'to promote...learning and glorify the works of God'. Enter the gardens through the stone arch on the High Street, named after the garden's benefactor, Lord Danby. Once inside, it is easy to navigate through the 5,000 species of plants housed in the glasshouses and surrounding gardens. Check the gardens' website for details of regular events like children's trails that keep any budding Alan Titchmarsh occupied for hours. *Adm (in summer & weekends).* Open daily 9am-4pm (Nov-Feb), 9am-5pm (Mar, Apr, Sep & Oct), 9am-6pm (May-Aug). Rose Ln, T: 01865 286690, www.botanic-garden.ox.ac.uk

Colleges

Christ Church College 5E

Christ Church can boast the largest quad, the grandest dining hall, the largest belled gatehouse, the only college whose chapel doubles as the city cathedral and the record for turning out the most Prime Ministers (13 and counting). Re-founded in 1546 by Henry VIII, the college houses the imposing Tom Tower, designed by Sir Christopher Wren and built in 1682 to safeguard the Great Tom bell. The 16th-century Great Hall *(see box p.4)*, reached by ascending a grand staircase, is decorated with portraits of significant college alumni like PM Gladstone, philosopher John Locke and writer Charles Dodgson a.k.a Lewis Carroll *(see box p.14)*. The Hall is closed to the public at mealtimes (usually between 12noon-2pm) so make sure you visit outside of these times to avoid disappointment.

Christ Church Cathedral 5E

The interior of this 12th-century cathedral could be said to reflect either a rich chapel or a poor man's cathedral following its promotion to the diocese of Oxford by Henry VIII in 1546. Take one of the guided tours to ensure you catch all the cathedral's best features including the shrine of Oxford's patron Saint Frideswide, the chancel vault with its stellar rib vaulting and the medieval Becket window, unfortunately minus Becket's face following defacement in the 16th century. *Adm.* Open 10am-4.15pm Mon-Sat, 2pm-4.15pm Sun (Cathedral closes at 4.45pm daily for choir practice). Public entrance is via the Meadow Building, St Aldate's, T: 01865 276492, www.chch.ox.ac.uk

Magdalen College 5G

Pronounced 'mawd-lin', this college is perhaps the most beautiful of the 38 colleges thanks largely to its 15th-century cloistered quad. Stop a while to admire the stone carved

Rowing boats at Magdalen Bridge

animals sitting aloft the buttresses in the tranquil courtyard. If you take the eastern passage out of the quad you'll find the River Cherwell running alongside the college walls. Cross the bridge and you can pick up Addison's Walk, a circular pathway that takes a worthwhile tour of the water meadow. Magdalen's famous Deer Park is also nearby where in winter or spring you may be lucky enough to spot one of its sixty strong herd of resident fallow deer. *Adm. Open daily 1pm-6pm or dusk (whichever is earlier) Oct-Jun, 12noon-7pm Jul-Sep. High St, T: 01865 276000, www.magd.ox.ac.uk*

Brasenose College 4E

Founded on the original site of Brasenose Hall, this college derives its name from the brass nose-shaped knocker that once adorned the Hall. This precious knocker now hangs behind the high table in the Hall where it was mounted upon its return to the college after a rebellion to start a rival college saw it taken to Lincolnshire. The nose motif can be seen throughout the college, most notably in the stonework surrounding the main gate. You may also recognise the grand High Street frontage of the college as 'Lonsdale College' in the *Inspector*

Brasenose College quad

Morse TV series (*see p.30*). *Adm. For exact opening times contact T: 01865 277830, Radcliffe Square. www.bnc.ox.ac.uk*

Students head to the Sheldonian theatre for their matriculation ceremony

Canterbury Quad in St John's College

All Souls College 4E

Unlike the rest of the collegiate, All Souls only admits graduate students based on examination, invitation or competition and as such represents the epitome of scholarly devotion. It is strange then that the brainiest of Oxford choose to parade around the college grounds at midnight carrying a dead duck on a pole and singing the Mallard song. Luckily this only happens every hundred years on January 14th to commemorate the day a huge mallard was discovered by workmen while laying the college foundations.

The next hunt will be in 2101 so in the meantime why not admire Hawksmoor's grand 'ivory towers' or the sundial designed by Sir Christopher Wren on the wall of the Codrington Library. *Adm free. Open 2pm-4pm Mon-Fri. High St, T: 01865 279379, www.all-souls.ox.ac.uk*

Spectacular spires of All Souls College

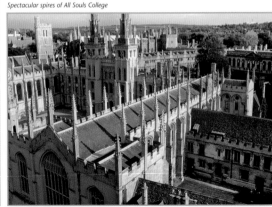

Merton College 5F

Founded in 1264, Merton still grapples with University (**4F**) and Balliol (**4D**) over the 'oldest college' status but it can certainly claim the 'oldest quad' title with its completion of Mod Quad in 1378. It also houses the oldest academic library in the world and the only one in Oxford

Entrance to Merton College

open to the public, allowing you the chance to view a first edition of *The Canterbury Tales* preserved within. *Adm. Open 2pm-5pm Mon-Fri, 10am-5pm Sat-Sun. Merton St, T: 01865 276310, www.merton.ox.ac.uk*

Other Colleges well worth a visit:

St John's College 3D

Undoubtedly the richest college in Oxford, St John's reflects this wealth through its extensive grounds and immaculate tended gardens. *Adm. Open daily 1-5pm. St. Giles St, T: 01865 277300, www.sjc.ox.ac.uk*

New College 4F

Built on a plague burial ground, New's highlights include the chapel's west window designed by Sir Joshua Reynolds. *Adm free in winter. Open daily 11am-5pm Mar-early Oct, 2pm-4pm rest of the year. Holywell St, T: 01865 279253, www.new.ox.ac.uk*

Exeter College 4E

Recognisable as the place where TV's Inspector Morse suffered his heart attack (*see p.30*), Exeter also boasts a Victorian chapel modelled on Paris' *Sainte-Chapelle*. *Adm free. Open daily 2pm-5pm. Turl St, T: 01865 279600, www.exeter.ox.ac.uk*

Bridge of Sighs, Hertford College

Hertford College 4E

One of the most photographed colleges thanks to the bridge connecting two of the college buildings, known popularly as the 'Bridge of Sighs' after the *Ponte dei Sospiri* in Venice. *Closed to the public. Catte St, T: 01865 279400, www.hertford.ox.ac.uk*

Jesus College 4D

For over 400 years this college has been a haven for the Welsh with a succession of Welsh Principals. *Adm. Open daily 2pm-4.30pm. Turl St, T: 01865 279700, www.jesus.ox.ac.uk*

Buy it

Shopping is not perhaps the first thing that springs to mind when you think of this historic city but, aside from the usual high street suspects found along Cornmarket Street and the nearby shopping centres, it is in the plentiful supply of independent retailers where Oxford really comes up trumps. The city offers a cornucopia of produce from embroidered college clothing to curious *Alice in Wonderland* memorabilia, delectable Oxford Blue cheese sold under the ancient Covered Market to bespoke leather brogues at Duckers & Son. You may find that with this many irresistible shops spread about the place, any efforts to limit the inevitable compulsion to souvenir shop will fall well and truly by the wayside.

Areas

Centre 5D

The best place to start is in the heart of the shopping district at Carfax Tower *(see p.3)*. From here the crossroads of Queen St, High St, Cornmarket St and St Aldate's offer even the most demanding shopper everything from well-known high street and designer stores to independent gift and curiosity shops.

Westgate Oxford 5C

Currently closed for major renovation, it will reopen in Autumn 2017 with a new cinema and flagship John Lewis anchor store. Castle St, T: 01865 725455, www.westgateoxford.co.uk

Clarendon Centre 4D

This shopping centre has the usual high street names such as Zara, Gap, Office and French Connection. *Open daily 8am-6pm Mon-Sat, 10am-5pm Sun. 8am-7pm Thur.* 52 Cornmarket St, T: 01865 251493, www.clarendoncentre.co.uk

University of Oxford shop

High Street 5D-5G

Thankfully the number of chain stores has been restricted on this historic street leaving the High open to a range of specialist independent retailers.

University of Oxford shop 5E

As the official merchandiser for the University of Oxford, they stock a large range of college strips so even if you're not a fully-fledged member of the rowing team you can always pretend. 106 High St, T: 01865 247414, www.oushop.com

St Aldate's 5D-6D

Alice's Shop 6D

All fans of Lewis Carroll's *Through the Looking Glass* should make a pilgrimage to this tiny shop where the real life Alice Liddell used to buy her sweets back in the 1830s. Apparently the bleating voice of the shopkeeper inspired Carroll to feature the shop and its resident 'sheep' keeper (*see p.14*). Crammed full of

Alice's Shop

Alice memorabilia, this curiosity shop of souvenirs and collectables will marvel even the biggest Alice aficionado.

83 St Aldate's, T: 01865 723793, www.aliceinwonderlandshop.com

Turl Street 4E

This crooked pedestrian street winds past a number of colleges and connects Broad and High Streets making it a popular choice for quickly crossing the centre, particularly for students late for tutorials – so watch out for them flying past on bicycles. A number of upmarket shops line this popular thoroughfare, from antique, book and whisky shops to traditional men's outfitters.

Ducker & Sons 4E

Founded in 1898, this bespoke shoemaker is an institution amongst Oxford's elite. Past customers include J.R.R. Tolkien, Evelyn Waugh and a host of Maharajahs. If you're in the market for some works of

Traditional shoemaking at Ducker & Sons

art doubling as shoes then look no further. *6 Turl St, T: 01865 242461, www.duckerandson.co.uk*

Broad Street 4D-4E

X marks the spot on this street where Oxford Martyrs Nicholas Ridley, Hugh Latimer and Thomas Cranmer were burnt at the stake for heresy in the 16th century (*see the larger Martyrs' Memorial on St Giles St* **4D**). Now it's home to a host of book and music shops, college gift shops and Boswells department store.

Blackwell's bookshop

Boswells 4D

Established in 1738, Oxford's only independent department store is well worth a visit for a little 'are you being served' old school charm. *Open daily 9.30am-6pm Mon-Fri, 9am-6pm Sat, 11am-5pm Sun. 1-4 Broad St, T: 01865 241244 www.boswells.co.uk*

Blackwell's 4E

One of Oxford's gems, this flagship bookshop has resided on Broad Street since its opening in 1879 and has been expanding up, down, and side to side ever since, making book browsing here a real 'tardis' experience. *48-51 Broad St, T: 01865 792792, www.blackwells.co.uk*

Walton Street and Little Clarendon Street 2B-3C

A little further out from the city centre, Little Clarendon Street links St Giles to Walton Street, which lies at the heart of the bohemian and stylish district of Jericho. Independent clothing and jewellery boutiques line this stretch alongside gift and homeware stores, and antique and second-hand bookshops; perfect if you prefer a little individuality.

Markets

The Covered Market 4D

Created in 1772 in an effort to tidy up the city and consolidate the sprawling outdoor meat markets around Carfax, the Covered Market has been doing a roaring trade

Alice's Adventures in Oxford

Charles Dodgson was a mathematics don at Christ Church college *(see p.8)* but gained notoriety as his alter ego, Lewis Carroll when the stories he invented to entertain the College Dean's daughter Alice Liddell *(see p.13)* and her sisters were later published as *Alice's Adventures in Wonderland* and *Through the Looking Glass*. References to his literary characters can be found across the city, particularly in the stained-glass windows of Christ Church College Hall and on its brass firedogs whose elongated necks mimic Alice's misfortune. The very dodo that inspired Dodgson to include the odd creature in his tales can still be seen in the Natural History Museum *(see p.5)*, although only the mummified head and foot survive today.

Famous Oxford Blue

ever since. Now, in addition to the competing smells from traditional cheesemakers, butchers, bakers, fishmongers and greengrocers, a host of gift shops and cafés trade here too, giving the market its distinctive fusion of old and new. *Open 8am-5.30pm Mon-Sat, 10am-4pm Sun. High St, www.oxford-coveredmarket.co.uk*

The Oxford Cheese Shop 4D

This popular cheesemaker has been resident in the market since the early 1980s and stocks some 250-plus varieties of cheese including the Oxford Isis and the award-winning Oxford Blue. *Avenue 1, 17 Covered Market, T: 01865 721420, oxfordcheese.co.uk*

David John Butchers 4D

A longstanding butchers with a sterling reputation for producing fine sausages and delectable pies. *Avenue 3, 93-95 Covered Market, T: 01865 249092*

Bitten Street Market 5C

This seasonal street food market is a great place to find a tasty range of street food on the run *(see p. 24).* *Open 11.30am-3.30pm, 1st Saturday of the month (Mar-Oct) www.bittenoxford.co.uk*

Covered Market

Gloucester Green 4C

An open-air market runs here every Wednesday *(9am-4pm)* offering a colourful display of fruit and veg alongside odds and ends stalls. There is also an antique and crafts market held every Thursday *(9am-4pm).*

A traditional **Farmers Market** runs here the first and third Thursday of every month *(9am-2pm)*, with stalls from local producers selling vegetables, meat, fish, bread, preserves and dairy products.

Watch it

For years Oxford has been a breeding ground for college luvvies treading the boards and thankfully this flair for the arts has led to a flourishing theatre and music scene with numerous venues across the city dedicated to the cause. As such Oxford has earned a reputation for producing quality theatre from mainstream to the avant-garde, wide-ranging cinema to suit cult film buffs and blockbuster diehards, nightclubs to indulge all dance tastes from body breaking to dad dancing, and a truly eclectic mix of live music from classical right through to head-banging rock. No better are these talents demonstrated than through the annual Oxfringe fringe festival, proving that for an ancient city Oxford has a thoroughly modern take on entertainment.

What's on?

Look out for *In Oxford*, Oxford's foremost tourist magazine for entertainment listings found free in hotels, restaurants, and most tourist attractions. Check out their website for full listings at:
www.inoxford.co.uk

The **Daily Info** website remains Oxford's most popular online listings guide, providing an up-to-date entertainment directory for live music, theatre and comedy, plus useful independent reviews:
www.dailyinfo.co.uk

Local newspapers
The Oxford Times
www.oxfordtimes.co.uk
Oxford Mail, *www.oxfordmail.co.uk*

Annual Events

Cowley Road Carnival 1H-3H & 5H
Popular celebration of multicultural Oxford in July (*see box p.17*). *Cowley Rd, www.cowleyroadcarnival.co.uk*

Dragon fever at Cowley Road Carnival

Encaenia
With great pomp and circumstance, honorary degree recipients, University dignitaries and Heads of Colleges walk in procession to the Sheldonian Theatre (**4E**) for the Encaenia ceremony in June (*see p.7*).

Oxfringe
Running since 2007, Oxford's first fringe festival is dedicated to music, literature, comedy and theatre. Its two-week long programme is hosted at various venues across the city. *Check oxfordfringe.org for festival dates and a full programme.*

Oxford Literary Festival 5E

Held annually in multiple venues within the city towards the end of March, this festival attracts the *crème de la crème* of literary society with a series of talks, workshops and readings. You can book tickets in advance online or by phone or purchase on the day from the box office marquee.
T: 0870 343 1001,
oxfordliteraryfestival.org

Torpids and Eights Week

Annual inter-collegiate rowing races held on the River Isis (**6D-6A**) in February and May. Due to

Torpid racing on the River Isis

the narrowness of the river and the number of colleges entered, a system of 'bumping' is used where boats line up one in front of the other and attempt to catch and 'bump' the boat in front of them to win the race.

St Giles' Fair 3D

(*See box p.19*) *T: 01865 249811, www.oxford.gov.uk*

Arts Centres

03 Gallery 5C

This modern venue located in the Oxford Castle complex displays a range of selling exhibitions from regional artists. *Oxford Castle, T: 01865 246131, www.o3gallery.co.uk*

The Jam Factory 4A

This arts centre-cum-restaurant displays regular exhibitions by local artists, in addition to running workshops and classes, making it *the* place to appreciate creativity and coffee in equal measures.

27 Park End St, T: 01865 244613, www.thejamfactoryoxford.com

The North Wall Off map at 1C

The focus of this theatre, art gallery and studios is on new and innovative work. Expect *avant-garde* theatre, comedy and much more. *South Parade, T: 01865 319450, www.thenorthwall.com*

Cinemas

Odeon 4C & 4D

Spread over two venues, expect the usual big screen listings from this national cinema chain. *George St* and Magdalen St, T: 0333 006 7777 (online booking only), www.odeon.co.uk

Phoenix Picture House 2B
Superb arthouse theatre showing a good balance of mainstream and independent film. 57 Walton St, T: 871 902 5736, www.picturehouses.com

Ultimate Picture Palace 2H & 6H
Oxford's only independently run cinema, this single-screen venue

Phoenix Picture House

is an institution for dedicated film buffs, showing a virtual smorgasbord of film, everything from classic to international titles and cult cinema. Jeune St (off Cowley Rd), T: 01865 245288, www.uppcinema.com

Comedy Club

The Glee Club 4B
This chain comedy store runs quality stand-up gigs from a variety of local and touring comedians. Hythe Bridge St, T: 0871 472 0400, www.glee.co.uk

Clubs

Lava Ignite 4B
Expect long queues to Oxford's premier nightclub. With three dance floors, five bars and regular themed nights from cheesy pop and trance to hip hop and RnB, Lava Ignite is certainly popular with the locals and students alike. Cantay House, Park End St, T: 01865 250181, www.lavaignite.com

Laughter central at The Glee Club

Ropponngi 4C
Ropponi is named after the high-class area of Tokyo and caters for the discerning of Oxford. Small but packed with sparkle and glitz, this lounge club is perfect for cocktails and celebrations. 29 George St, T: 01865 241 574, www.roppongi-oxford.com

The Bridge 4B
A tad classier than Lava Ignite, this polished club has regular student nights although 'pure bridge' night every Saturday is a big crowd-puller for all, with cheesy tunes and RnB spread over two floors. 6-9 Hythe

Fun of the fair

Originally a religious event dating from 1624, the **St Giles' Fair** was soon adopted by the city as a perfect opportunity for a local shindig and is now held annually on St Giles Street (**3D**) on the first Monday and Tuesday in September. Progress has seen the popular Victorian freak shows, theatre and lady-wrestling replaced with high-tech rides, video games and amusements but the essence of the fair remains in all its candy-flossed glory.

*Bridge St, T: 01865 242526,
www.bridgeoxford.co.uk*

Live Music

The Bullingdon 3H & 6H

Enjoy regular live music nights here including 'Backroom' Fridays where all the wedding disco-style tunes are played and Jazz night Tuesdays. *162 Cowley Rd, T: 01865 244516, www.thebullingdon.co.uk*

The Cellar 4D

A key venue for alternative live music, with regular indie, hip hop and electro nights. *Fewin Court (Off Cornmarket St), T: 01865 244761, www.cellaroxford.co.uk*

The Jericho Tavern 2B

Famous for showcasing Oxford's finest bands, this trendy pub on Walton Street features a range of gigs and DJs for all tastes. *56 Walton St, T: 01865 311775, www.thejerichooxford.co.uk*

The Wheatsheaf 5E

Small venue running regular live music nights from rock to indie and hosts of *The Spin - Oxford's Jazz Club* who play Thursday nights throughout the year. *129 High St, T: 01865 721156*

O2 Academy Oxford 3H & 6H

This is undoubtedly Oxford's leading live music and club venue thanks to its O2 Academy ownership, making it a regular date on the playing circuit for leading rock, indie and alternative music bands. *190 Cowley Rd, T: 0905 0203999, Box Office T: 08444 77 2000 www.o2academyoxford.co.uk*

Holywell Music Room 3E

Performances here benefit from the beautiful surrounds and excellent acoustics of this purpose-built concert hall dating from 1742. Classical concerts are held here most

Jericho Tavern

Music Listings

Nightshift is a free monthly magazine available at most music venues, giving comprehensive gig listings. *www.nightshiftmag.co.uk*

For further music listings check out:
www.inoxford.com
www.dailyinfo.co.uk

Classical concert schedules can be found at:
www.musicatoxford.com
www.coffeeconcerts.co.uk

Sundays at 11.15am as part of the Oxford Coffee Concert events, which continue to be one of the most successful chamber music series in the country. *Tickets are available from the Oxford Playhouse box office (see p.21) or by T: 01865 305305, Holywell St, www.coffeeconcerts.co.uk*

Sheldonian Theatre 4E
Designed by Sir Christopher

Wren before he created St Paul's Cathedral, the Sheldonian was modelled on the open air theatre of Marcellus in Rome, although the Oxford rain required a roof. In addition to its use as the venue for *Encaenia (see p.16)* and degree ceremonies, the theatre hosts numerous classical music concerts from international orchestras to individual artists. *Tickets are available online from www.musicatoxford.com, T: 01865 244806 or from the Oxford Playhouse box office (see p.21).*

Sheldonian Theatre

Open Air Theatre

Experience Shakespeare in atmospheric surrounds such as the college gardens or Oxford Castle with productions from the **Creation Theatre Company** and the **Oxford Shakespeare Company**.
www.creationtheatre.co.uk
www.oxfordshakespearecompany.co.uk

The theatre is also open to visitors outside of ceremonial, meeting and concert use. *Adm. Open 10am-4.30pm Mon-Sat, 10am-3pm Mon-Sat (Dec-Jan) 10am-4.30pm Sun (May-Sep). Broad St, T: 01865 277299, www.sheldon.ox.ac.uk*

Theatres

Burton Taylor Studio Theatre 4C
Named after actors Richard Burton and Elizabeth Taylor, this intimate 50-seater theatre offers a range of innovative and experimental student theatre throughout term time and community theatre/visiting productions the rest of the year. *All tickets available from the Oxford Playhouse box office, Gloucester St, T: 01865 305305, www.oxfordplayhouse.com*

New Theatre Oxford 4C
This is the place to go to for musical theatre, comedy and gigs. Its 1,800-seat capacity makes it the largest commercial theatre in Oxford and a regular venue for national touring shows. *George St, T: 0844 871 3020, www.atgtickets.com/venues/new-theatre-oxford*

Oxford Playhouse 4C
The city's premier arts theatre, the Playhouse, leads the way with high calibre drama, dance, music, comedy and theatre. It plays host to visiting international productions, while also showcasing material from new playwrights and actors. *11-12 Beaumont St, T: 01865 305305, www.oxfordplayhouse.com*

The play's the thing...
The **Oxford University Dramatic Society (OUDS)** enjoys one of the most vibrant student drama scenes in England thanks to the large assembly of talent on offer from Oxford's collegiate, and its notable reputation for producing famous past members like Richard Burton, Dudley Moore, Rowan Atkinson, Hugh Grant and Sir John Gielgud. Check out full theatre listings at: *www.ouds.org*

Pegasus Theatre 6H
The Pegasus offers a great venue for a variety of performances including their specialist collaborations between young people and professional artists. The main Pullman Stage is named after their major supporter and patron Philip Pullman, whose trilogy *His Dark Materials* took inspiration for some its parallel universe settings from the city. *Magdalen Rd, T: 01865 812150, www.pegasustheatre.org.uk*

Pegasus Theatre interior

Taste it

Catering for a stack of hungry and thirsty students, dons, locals and international tourists would normally see the chef and the barman running for the door but luckily Oxford is made of sterner stuff. In fact with a mind-boggling array of restaurants, cafés, pubs and bars, the city not only accepts the challenge but surpasses expectation, offering a quality selection of food from traditional English fare through to the international delights of Lebanese, Italian, Thai, Turkish, Greek, Indian and Bangladeshi to name just a few. Not to be outdone, there exists an equally long list of ale houses, wine bars and pubs allowing you to whet your whistle whenever and wherever the mood takes you except perhaps when you're 'messing around on the river'.

Price Guide

Prices are for a full meal for one without alcohol.
£ = less than £10
££ = between £10 and £25
£££ = more than £25

Cafés

George & Danver (G & D's) £ 5D
Amazing ice-cream café where you'll happily queue for the delights of dimebar crunch, bananarama and oxford blue. They're always open to suggestions for new flavours so get

Fresh coffee from The Missing Bean

your creative juices flowing. *94 St. Aldate's, T: 01865 245952; 55 Little Clarendon St, T: 01865 516652; 104 Cowley Rd, T: 01865 727111, www.gdcafe.com*

The Missing Bean £ 4D
Coffee connoisseurs will not fail to be impressed by the blend range and quality of coffee on offer here, and with their own roastery, it's no wonder their java is sublime (the tea and hot choc is pretty good too). *14 Turl St, T: 01865 794886, www.themissingbean.co.uk*

The Grand Café £-££ 4F
Built on the spot of England's first recorded coffee shop in 1650, this café can be quite pricey but worth it if you fancy high tea or a glass of champagne in an opulent setting. *84 High St, T: 01865 204463, www.thegrandcafe.co.uk*

Thirsty Meeples Café £ 4C
If you like a café with a twist then look no further than Thirsty Meeples, a quirky board game café in the

heart of the city. Pay a cover charge and choose from 2000+ games to play while enjoying a coffee or light bite. Perfect for the closet board game fanatic in us all. *99 Gloucester Green, T: 01865 244247, www.thirstymeeples.co.uk*

Vaults & Garden Café £ 4E

A fantastic little café, with vaulted ceiling next door to St Mary's Church (*see p.7*) serving simple, organic lunch and tea with an emphasis on fairtrade. The outdoor seating in the churchyard garden makes a charming backdrop for afternoon tea amongst a host of historic buildings. *St Mary's Church,*

Atmospheric dining at the Vaults Café

Grand pillars at the Grand Café

Radcliffe Sq, T: 01865 279112, www.thevaultsandgarden.com

Restaurants

Al-Shami ££ 3B

Tucked away from the main thoroughfare, this small Lebanese restaurant provides an exhaustive choice of dishes from Sujuq to Shawarma. If indecision gets the better of you try the set menu option; at around £15 per head, it's the best way to try a little of everything. *25 Walton Crescent, T: 01865 310066, www.al-shami.co.uk*

Brasserie Blanc ££-£££ 2B

Oxford adoptee Raymond Blanc brings gourmet French cuisine to Jericho within a relaxed and contemporary setting. Try the set lunch and dinner menus if you fancy sampling high quality food without breaking the bank or alternatively splash out on mind-blowing *à la carte* dishes. *71-72 Walton St, T: 01865 510999, www.brasserieblanc.com*

Chiang Mai Kitchen ££ 5D

With quality Thai dishes made from authentic ingredients, you can treat yourself to fine dining Southeast

Scrummy Street Food £ 5C

Like many other foodie cities, Oxford too has joined the trend for street food markets. **Bitten Street** opened for business in 2014 and has built up quite a following from its Oxford Castle site. It offers a whole range of rotating light bites from Tibetan dumplings and French raclette to old school puddings and gelato. Plus a resident DJ means you can devour treats with a background beat. *Open 11.30am-3.30pm, 1st Saturday of the month (Mar-Oct), www.bittenoxford.co.uk, @BittenOxford*

Waterfront dining at The Folly

Asian style in the splendid surrounds of this original Tudor building. *130A High St, Kemp Hall Passage T: 01865 202233, www.chiangmaikitchen.co.uk*

Chutneys Indian Brasserie ££ 4C

With not a roll of flock wallpaper in sight, this contemporary styled Indian, located right in the centre of town, makes for a perfect place to refuel while you're between sights. A favourite among Oxford's vegetarian crowd thanks to its

extensive Southern Indian veggie fare. *36 St Michael's St, T: 01865 724241, www.chutneysoxford.co.uk*

Edamamé £-££ 4F

Offering Japanese home cooking just like mama Murakami used to make, Edamamé is great for affordable lunchtime stir-fries and noodles, with a more extensive evening menu on Friday and Saturdays. Don't miss sushi and sashimi night every Thursday. *No booking permitted and limited opening times so check in advance. 15 Holywell St, T: 01865 246916, www.edamame.co.uk*

Fishers ££-£££ Off map at 5H

Comfortably the best fish and seafood restaurant in Oxford with a great reputation for fresh quality produce on a daily changing menu. Its large and versatile menu caters for those on a budget with set lunch and early evening menus, plus *à la carte* for those wanting to splurge on fresh lobster or seasonal fish. *36-37 St Clements, T: 01865 243003, www.fishers-restaurant.com*

Atomic Burger £ 2H & 6H

Head here for a nostalgic trip back to the 1980s with sci-fi, pop and TV references surrounding you as you chow down on themed burgers and hot dogs.
92 Cowley Rd, T: 01865 790855, www.atomicburger.co.uk

Kazbar £-££ 1H & 6H

Mezze and tapas-lovers flock here nightly to soak up some of the lantern-lit atmosphere and sangria in Cowley's very own Moroccan haven. Dishes start at around £3-4 but be warned that with tapas this good, one generally follows another and another. *25-27 Cowley Rd,*

Delicious fish dish from Malmaison

Food artwork at Shanghai 30s

T: 01865 202920, www.kazbar.co.uk

Malmaison Brasserie ££-£££ 5C

Converted from the local prison, this hotel brasserie has bags of character, making a quirky backdrop for lunch or dinner. *Oxford Castle, 3 New Rd, T: 084469 30659, www.malmaison.com*

The Folly ££-£££ 6D

This restaurant is all about location, location, location and great seasonal food of course. Set right alongside the River Isis, you can relax and relish sumptuous seafood and hearty meat dishes while passing rowers do all the hard work. *1 Folly Bridge, T: 01865 201293, www.the-folly.co.uk*

Shanghai 30's ££ 6D

Step inside this 15th-century building and be transported to swinging Shanghai thanks to atmospheric background jazz and period style furnishings. Add to this ambience, delicious and lovingly presented Chinese dishes from dim sum to sea-spiced chicken for an altogether authentic experience.
82 St Aldate's, T: 01865 242230, www.shanghai30s.com

Quod £-£££ 4E

Adjoining the Old Bank Hotel, this chic brasserie has everything covered from breakfast brunches to evening meals and afternoon tea. Sleek

Quod Brasserie

Rooftop dining at The Dining Room

service and quality cooking make it a great central option.
92-94 High St, T: 01865 202505,
www.quod.co.uk

The Ashmolean Dining Room £-££ 3C
Head chef Alun Roberts has created an eclectic European inspired menu, sourcing much of his ingredients from Oxfordshire suppliers. The restaurant's setting on the rooftop of the Ashmolean Museum makes it a great location to eat and enjoy the classic spires of Oxford from on high. *Ashmolean Museum, Beaumont St, T: 01865 553823, www.ashmoleandiningroom.com*

Pubs and Bars

Duke of Cambridge 2C
There are Mojitos and Cosmopolitans aplenty in this trendy cocktail bar. The happy hours between 5pm-9pm Sun-Thurs and 5pm-7.30pm Fri-Sat allow you to sample most of the cocktails at half price. *5-6 Little Clarendon St, T: 01865 558173, www.dukebar.com*

Freud 2B
This bar is worth a visit purely to experience the sinfulness of drinking within the cavernous surrounds of a converted Greek Revival Church. Check out their extensive cocktail and food menu including yummy homemade pizzas. *119 Walton St, T: 01865 311171, www.freud.eu*

Lamb & Flag 3D
Nearly opposite the Eagle and Child, this historic public house also boasts its fair share of literary connections. Thomas Hardy is said to have written parts of his last novel *Jude the Obscure* while supping on his pint at this very pub. *12 St Giles, T: 01865 515787*

The Bear Inn 5E
One of Oxford's oldest pubs, dating back to 1242, The Bear is perfect for

Cosmopolitan anyone?

The Lamb & Flag sign

a sneaky drink while shopping off the High. Look out for its impressive collection of ties given by customers over the years in exchange for a pint. *6 Alfred St, T: 01865 728164, www.bearoxford.co.uk*

The Big Society 2H

A relative newcomer to Oxford, this pub has already carved an impressive niche in the eclectic Cowley Road offering. Serving a range of American style bar food and complete with ping pong and table football, it's a big hit with the student crowd.
95 Cowley Rd, T: 01865 792755, www.bigsocietyoxford.com

The Eagle & Child 3C

Nicknamed the 'Bird and Baby', this small 17th-century pub is always popular thanks largely to its past literary clientele so be prepared to stay standing at the weekends (*see box right*). *49 St Giles, T: 01865 302925*

Turf Tavern 4F

A favourite with both town and gown, the Turf is tucked behind the city walls, making it a little harder to find but well worth the hunt. Low beamed ceilings and a warren of hideyholes provide a cosy place to

The Eagle and Child sign

sample a huge selection of ales and cider on tap.
4-5 Bath Place, T: 01865 243235, www.theturftavern.co.uk

The Head of the River 6E

The perfect watering hole for a post-punting drink right by the river. *1 Folly Bridge, T: 01865 721600, www.headoftheriveroxford.co.uk*

The Inklings

With a membership list that reads like a who's who of fantasy literature, the Inklings literary group met at the Eagle and Child pub (*see left*) between the 1930s and 1960s. C.S. Lewis author of *The Lion, the Witch and the Wardrobe* and J.R.R.Tolkien, author of the *Lord of the Rings* trilogy and *The Hobbit* were regular attendees as the plaque and signed letter from them testify in the pub's 'rabbit room' where they congregated regularly for meetings.

taste it

Know it

Thanks to its central location, Oxford is well served by road and rail networks, with regular links to London Gatwick and Heathrow Airports allowing local, national and international access. Boasting the UK's first park and ride scheme, the city's public transport system works well within a challenging labyrinth of old streets and one-way systems.

By far the greenest and most pleasant way to see Oxford is on foot and with a variety of tours on offer you are spoilt for choice (see p.30). Alternatively grab a bike and join the speeding students on the shortcut back alleys that criss-cross the city, or hit the water, preferably in a punt, and enjoy Oxford's lazy waterways at a more relaxed pace.

Tourist Information Centre (TIC) 4D
Open 9.30am-5.30pm Mon-Sat (5pm in winter), 10am-4pm Sun (3.30pm in winter).
15-16 Broad St, T: 01865 686430, www.visitoxfordandoxfordshire.com

Arriving

By Coach

Oxford Bus Company 4C
The Airline service departs from Gloucester Green bus station. It runs every 30 minutes to Heathrow and hourly to Gatwick Airports. *T: 01865 785400, www.oxfordbus.co.uk*

Oxford Tube 4C
Offers regular express coach services to London's Victoria coach and railway station. *T: 01865 772250, www.oxfordtube.com*

By Train

Oxford Train Station 4A
Links to nationwide destinations.

T: 03457 484950, www.nationalrail.co.uk

Getting Around

Bus

Gloucester Green Bus and Coach Station 4C

Oxford Bus Company
A day pass ticket allows unlimited travel within the Oxford Smart Zone. An All Zones 'Go Anywhere' day pass allows unlimited travel within the city and to surrounding towns like Abingdon, Didcot and Wallingford. *T: 01865 785400, www.oxfordbus.co.uk*

Open-top bus tour

Stagecoach

Dayrider tickets give unlimited day travel within Oxford.
T: 01865 772250,
www.stagecoachbus.com/oxfordshire
For real time bus departure information check out: www.oxontime.com

Taxi

You will find the main taxi ranks located at Gloucester Green (**4C**), the railway station (**4A**) and St Giles Street (**3D**).

Car

Driving in the city centre can be difficult due to congestion from a number of one-way systems and access restrictions on its main thoroughfares. It is far better to take advantage of Oxford's excellent Park and Ride facilities instead.

Park and Ride

With five locations at redbridge, thornhill, pear tree, water eaton and seacourt you can access the

Bikes galore on Broad Street

city from all directions. *A return to the city centre starts from £2.80 and additional car parking fees apply at pear tree, redbridge and seacourt.*
T: 01865 785400,
parkandride.oxfordbus.co.uk
If you do need to drive, the most convenient car parks for the city centre are:
Railway Station *(518 spaces)* **4A**
Worcester Street *(enter from Park End Street)* *(180 spaces)* **4B**
Gloucester Green *(104 spaces)* **4C**
Oxpens - temporary car park until 2017 *(420 spaces)* **4A**

Bicycle Hire

Cycloanalysts 3H & 6H

150 Cowley Rd, T: 01865 424444, www.cycloanalysts.com

Bike Zone 4D

28-32 St Michael St, T: 01865 728877, www.bike-zone.co.uk

Boat and Punt Hire

Cherwell Boathouse Off map at 3H

Hires punts, rowing boats and canoes alongside a top notch English fare restaurant and bar so you can work off any indulgence.
Bardwell Rd, T: 01865 515978, www.cherwellboathouse.co.uk

Magdalen Bridge Boathouse 5G

Punts, pedaloes and rowing boats all available for hire from Magdalen Bridge. *Old Horse Ford, High St, T: 01865 202643, www.oxfordpunting.co.uk*

To punt or not to punt?

If you really want the full Oxford experience then you must give punting a bash. Successful punting is all about balance and making full use of the pole both to propel and steer you along by feeding it through your hands as you push it into the water.

With technique mastered you're free to explore: from the Cherwell Boathouse turn downstream to float alongside the University Parks (**1G**) and Parson's Pleasure (once a nude sunbathing hang-out for the local gentry **2H**). Alternatively from Magdalen Bridge (**5G**) you can punt past the Botanic Garden (**5G**) and St Hilda's College (**6H**) heading onwards up the byways to the River Isis. Punts are available to hire *(see p.29)* from mid-March to mid-October, 10am-dusk.

Just messing around on the river...

Salter's Steamers 6D

With over 150 years of nautical experience, Salter's hires punts, rowing and motorboats to take on the River Thames. They also run cruises if you'd prefer someone else to do the hard work. *Folly Bridge, T: 01865 243421, www.salterssteamers.co.uk*

Tours

Walking Tours

Official walking tours of the city conducted by Blue or Green Badge guides leave the TIC *(see box p.28)* throughout the day (check website for times). For details on specialist tour subjects like film locations for *Inspector Morse (see p.9 and p.11)*, architecture, literary figures and historical periods, pick up a leaflet from the TIC or see details online: *www.visitoxfordandoxfordshire.com*

DIY Walking Tours

mp3 guided walking tours allow you to navigate the city at your own pace. Try downloading from *www.tourist-tracks.com*